I0479654

The Quick Guide to Entrepreneurship

A Handbook for Beginners

By Zach Reyes

Essential Habits for Success 7

Getting enough sleep 9

Rise Early 10

How to Become a Morning Person 12

Regular Exercise 14

Eat a Proper Breakfast 16

Meditation 18

Never stop learning 20

Make a Business Journal 22

Goal Setting 25

Defining you Goals 27

Formulating Smart Goals 29

Why People Fail 31

Your Business Plan 35

Essential Knowledge 37

Overcoming Obstacles 38

Developing a Plan 40

Business Plan Timeline 42

Designing Your Business Plan 44

Overcome the Fear of Acting 46

The First Step 48

Time Management 51

Coordinate Your Day 54

Prioritize and make a To-Do list 56

Know When to Delegate 58

Take Frequent Breaks 60

Productivity 63

Avoiding Procrastination 65

Self-Discipline 66

Focus 67

Tools and Apps to Increase your Productivity 68

Personal Notes 72

As an entrepreneur, you are always on a roller coaster ride.

You will have a lot of up and downs and go from euphoria to torment very fast. Being an entrepreneur is all about learning to navigate these ups and downs so that you will succeed in the end.

You will hear about lucky people and who, in the blink of an eye, went from nothing to everything. Know that these cases are few and far between. Most people need to rely on hard work and grit to get where they want. It is not always a smooth ride, but it can be a very rewarding one.

To succeed as an entrepreneur, you need to be motivated. Motivation gives you the self-confidence to look forward and dream big! Motivation is the force that drives you forward and enables you to make the right decision every single day.

It is easy to linger in our comfort zone, to play within our limits, and never take the leap. All you have in the comfort zone is hope. A hope that one day you will miraculously succeed where others have failed. Hope is a great motivator, but a lousy tactic. Therefore, you need to step out of your comfort zone and take a peek at what lies beyond. You need to face discomfort, fear of failure, and possible humiliation.

For most people, the road to success is not a straight line, but a twisted and tumultuous path with plateaus and setbacks. What really counts, in the long run, is that you continue to improve yourself little by little every day. That you hold yourself accountable and don't blame others when you make a mistake (You will.). If you keep yourself responsible for every mistake that you made, you will learn from it and improve.

Learning the fundamentals of entrepreneurship is your first step towards achieving your dream.

Apply and build upon the principles that you learn in this book, work hard and stay the course, and one day you'll get there!

Chapter 1

Essential Habbits for Success

To become successful, you must be able to adapt and learn new things to stay ahead of the competition. You must be a visionary, be able to identify an opportunity when you see one and act on it!

You must be ready to face the fear of uncertainty and potential failure while taking deliberate risks and leaps of faith.

You will fall, but whats matters is how many times you get up again. How many times you brush off the dirt and venture on. How you deal with failure is what sets you apart from other entrepreneurs.

Commitment and a high level of determination is what will make you succeed in the end. You must be passionate and self-disciplined enough to maintain the motivation to do what is needed off you.

Hard work beats talent any day, and success is the end result of all the small things you do every day.

In this chapter, we will look at the foundation. The daily habits and traits that define every successful entrepreneur.

Get Enough Sleep

For most people, it is advised to get 7-9 hours of sleep every night. Any less, and you'll rapidly feel depleted during the day, and your creativity and concentration will take a severe plunge.

Night owls may be creative. However, in the long run, well-rested people will stay more focused and therefore increasingly profitable. Entrepreneurs that want to succeed should dump the late-night sessions and hit the bed on time to get enough sleep.

The following method might help you find out how many hours of sleep you need:

- Set your desired wakeup time, and count back 8 hours, and use that time as your bedtime for 5 days.
- After 5 days, if you're not waking up a few minutes before the alarm goes off, push your bedtime back half an hour for another 5 days.
- Keep On adjusting your bedtime until you can wake up without your alarm.

You'll know that you have found your perfect bedtime when you can complete everything you need before work, and still don't feel that you rushed through the morning.

Rise early!

Being an entrepreneur, your day is filled with meetings and a multitude of different tasks, and you might feel that there are never enough hours in the day. Veteran entrepreneurs know that they should get up early in the morning to get the most out of their day.

Getting up early gives you a head start to your day. By getting up earlier than your competitors, you have a chance to exercise, eat a decent breakfast, and go through all your arrangements before most people even start their day.

Starting the day on the right foot can have a substantial effect on innovativeness and efficiency levels. Utilizing the early morning hours, a period of the day when there are fewer requests, is a sure way to get more done. Regardless of whether you are a morning person or not, you may have more self discipline in the early morning hours than later in the day.

To abstain from falling into an ineffective snare, it's critical to create a morning schedule that places you in the proper position to successfully conquer your day.

Throughout the day, as you're doing tasks, holding meetings, or taking requests, you utilize self-control, experience and abilities, causing you to feel drained towards the end of the day. In contrast, mornings offer you the chance to establish a positive footing for the rest of the day.

If you've at any point have overslept or forgotten your children's snack on the counter, you will know that starting your day with frustration can severely impact your efficiency at work. If you then wait until late in the evening to do your most crucial tasks, you are more likely to simply postpone them or rush through them poorly.

In the early morning hours, nobody is going to call or message you, there aren't any meetings, and there aren't e-mails streaming in and out. Since most people simply don't care about rising early, you get a head start and won't be disturbed by constant requests. You will be fully able to concentrate on the tasks and requirements that truly move the needle before all the challenges of an ordinary workday comes at you.

Since your morning routines influence your whole day. What you do or don't do every day will directly impact how profitable you are, how vigorous you feel, what you achieve, and, at last, how successful you will be as an entrepreneur.

How to be a morning person!

Adjusting to getting up early in the morning is not an easy task. If you abruptly go from getting up at 8 a.m. to setting your alarm at 5 a.m., you're positioning yourself for failure. Instead, use the following approach to gradually adjust your morning routine.

Start with baby steps!

Adjust your alarm little by little. If you're used to having your alarm at 07.30 a.m., move the alarm, in 15 minutes increments, towards your desired get-up time. This is a lot easier and less overwhelming than doing it all in a big jump.

Move the Alarm away from the bed!

Nearly all people read on their phones before going to sleep, and then set the alarm and put the phone on the nightstand. By having the phone close by, it is effortless to hit the snooze button again and again when the alarm goes off in the morning. Therefore, try to put your phone away from the bed before going to sleep.

If you find that standing up to put away the phone wakes you up, buy a cheap alarm clock instead (I promise you it is worth the investment) and set the alarm before you go to bed. By doing this, you are forced to get up when the alarm goes off. After a few drowsy mornings, getting up at the first bell will feel like second nature.

Get up and turn on the lights immediately!

Another method that supplements having the alarm a long way from the bed is getting up and turning on the lights straight away. As long as the lights are off, it is easy to just stay and cuddle in bed, but when you get up and turn on the lights directly after turning off the alarm, you are forced to stay awake.

Regular exercise

Remaining healthy is one of the best things you can do to support both your private and professional career. Regular exercise will make you both physically and mentally fit, which will improve your mood, help you sleep better, and boost your stamina. Training is, therefore, a sure way to increase work efficiency.

Exercise will:

- Give you a (well earned) sense of achievement, improve your physique, and give a boost to your self-esteem.

- Teach you to adhere to schedules and goals. By sticking to your workout schedule, you will achieve discipline that will carry over to your work life.

- Boost your productivity by releasing chemical compounds that improve your ability to focus and concentrate.

- Increase your metabolic rate and make you burn calories faster.

- Improve your sleep.

- Release endorphins, adrenaline, dopamine, and serotonin, all of which work together to boost your mood and decrease anxiety levels. Exercise can also reduce the amount of cortisol in the bloodstream, leading to a reduction of stress and lower blood pressure.

- Increases the size of the area in the brain involved in recollection and understanding.

- Help you break bad habits and make sure you'll stay competitive with others by challenging yourself and pushing your limits.

Your exercise should be something you enjoy and can be anything from running to you. It should be incorporated into your daily routine, but don't start with insane fitness plans that involve working out twice a day.

Start out with 15-20 minutes each day and increase the amount of training and intensity as you get into it. Be willing to see small improvements over time and don't burn out.

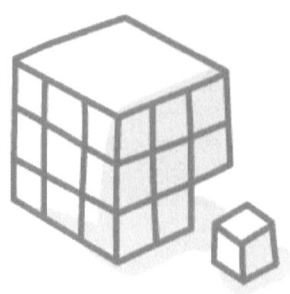

Eat a proper breakfast

Breakfast kick-starts your metabolism and provides the body and brain with much-needed fuel after an overnight fast.

An adequate breakfast restores glucose levels (a carbohydrate that is essential for the brain to function correctly). Consuming breakfast regularly every day can improve your memory and concentration while lowering your stress levels.

You don't need to eat a large meal, but you should take 5 to 10 minutes to prepare and consume a healthy breakfast within an hour of waking up.

Generally, you should eat a mix of foods that contains protein, carbohydrates, fiber, and healthy fats.

The carbs provide some much-needed energy right away, while the protein will last until lunch. Fiber-rich foods will keep you feeling full all morning. If you like, you can also drink a cup of coffee in the morning, but try to minimize the amount of caffeine you consume during the day.

You can try:

- A high-fiber cereal with fruits.
- Protein smoothie (low-fat) with oats and frozen fruits.
- Low-fat protein bars (when in a hurry).
- A yogurt and a glass of milk.

Try to drink atleast 8 cups of water every day. As a general rule, you should drink regularly enough so that you never feel thirsty.

If you feel that you need help with your diet, contact a dietitian to help you get back on track, or buy and use one of many Food Journals.

Meditation

As an entrepreneur, you will need to cope with risk, uncertainty and an ever-changing environment, but in the peacefulness of the morning, you have the opportunity to stop and relax. Nothing surpasses seeing the sky go from dim to light each day. Put aside some time to merely think. You could pause for a minute to consider every one of the things for which you are thankful before you start seeking new objectives. Practicing appreciation will give you more vitality, decrease tension, and make you increasingly optimistic about what's to come.

If you want to take it to the next level, you should look into meditation. Meditation is the discipline of focusing and redirecting your mind and can help you improve your attention span, reduce tension, and keep you calm in stressful environments.

Meditation can also improve your verbal and non-verbal reasoning and the ability to process information. This will increase your focus and enable you to react quickly to changes, both of which are extremely important in decision-making processes.

Below is a simple meditation exercise you can do right now:

1. Sit or lie comfortably.

2. Close your eyes.

3. Focus on your breathing slowly and naturally through your nose.

4. Extend your focus to your whole body and feel how the body moves with each inhalation and exhalation. Focus first on your feet, then your legs, your arms, and your torso. Relax each body part before continuing to the next one.

5. Lastly, focus on your head and mind. As you exhale, imagine that all stressful thoughts and doubts flow out your nose and that your mind empties. As you inhale, imagine that fresh air and calamity fills up your head.

Start with 2-3 minutes and when you feel like it, try for more extended periods.

Never stop learning!

New and innovational ideas are still just around the next corner, the world continuously evolves, and so should you. There is a reason why some of the most successful people in the world are those who are best at learning new skills and abilities.

By continuously learning, you will:

- Give you an array of perspectives to call on in your business pursuits.

- Build confidence as you master new-found knowledge and skills. This will make you more appealing to others because you will be able to adapt to new situations and excel in social settings.

- Think more creatively and improve your innovation.

You may have heard that the "brain is like muscle", and just like other muscles, you need to use it to improve it.

By learning something different every day (big or small), you hardwire your brain to stay engaged and receptive to new information. This will, in turn, improve your skill and knowledge base, and make you better at problem-solving and decision making.

Learning does not need to be strictly business-related but should be something that you enjoy and feel interested in.

There are several ways you can train your brain:

- Watch TED Talk videos.

- Use training apps on your mobile phone or tablet.

- Read your favorite publications.

- Learn a new language.

- Build your vocabulary.

- Browse Wikipedia.

Start Journaling!

Planning gives you the ability of foresight, enabling you to allocate resources for almost any eventuality. This is why innumerable entrepreneurs depend on everyday journaling. Some do it toward the beginning of the day. Others might want to write a diary in the evening.

Keeping a journal or a diary can be crucial to keep you grounded and on track as you face obstacles and tougher days.

When you record something, you will remember it better. Use your journal to take notes during meetings, thoughts and ideas throughout the day, feedback from others and your schedule. At regular intervals, peek back at your archives, and make new, improved notes.

Finish your day with 20 minutes of reflection and planning. Think about what you did best and what you could have done better. Write it down in your journal and try to apply the changes the next day.

Daily journaling is a powerful tool for proper Time Management and will help you keep perspective and control throughout your week.

Chapter 2

Defining your Goals

Proper goal setting is essential for every entrepreneur and enables you to achieve the results you want within a reasonable timeframe.

Professional goal setting means being smart about which goals you seek and how you choose to approach them.

Accomplishing your goals is all about your strategy and the capability to never quit.

Propper goals is the first step towards achievement and act as motivation in future endeavors.

In both short term and long term, goals are a representation of your dreams and give you a target to work towards.

By setting your goals, you set your heart and mind to a path towards future success.

Begin by formulating a business idea before assessing your current situation and resources to see how you will get there.

Defining your Goals

When formulating your goals you want to make sure that the goals are something you are passionate about and feel motivated to achieve. Moreover, you want the goals to be both realistic and achievable.

1. Visualization

The first and most important step is really to understand your goal (i.e., what you really want to achieve). Try to visualizing reaching your goal and which steps you needed to take in order to reach it.

2. Assess your current situation

Assess your current position. What advantages do you have (networks, contacts, finances,etc.)? Everybody has some advantages, and if you can't find yours, you need to analyze the situation more in-depth. At this point, you should also investigate how likely you are to reach your goals and possibly modify them (or find more middle goals) according to your current situation.

3. Make a long-term roadmap

Formulate a plan based on your current situation and which options are available to you. If you have made an honest assessment of yourself, you should be able to create a plan that appeals to your particular strengths and weaknesses, while taking into account possible obstacles you may meet on the way.

4. Divide your goals into smaller steps

When you know your goals and the overall plan, you need to split up your goals into smaller steps. You should separate your goals into daily, weekly, monthly and yearly goals (depending on how big your goal is). The point is that you create smaller, short term goals for every day or week. The smaller goals are also more measurable and can serve as a check to find out if you're on the right way.

People generally underestimate how long it takes to achieve things. Therefore, know that you are in for the long haul and that it will usually take some time before you see significant results.

Revisit your long-term roadmap every now and then to see if you're on the right track, or if you need to adjust your plan (or even the long-term goals themselves).

Regardless of how effective your plan is, there's always an opportunity to get better. For entrepreneurs, adapting to change never ends. Always look for tasks that take to long, or require unreasonably much work and attempt to improve or divide them into smaller and more manageable tasks. If you find that you have gotten into a dead end, and things obviously aren't working, readjust for goals or plans (sooner rather than later).

Formulation Goals - The ABCDE Method

When formulating your goals, use the SMART approach.

With the SMART approach, you break down and define each individual goal.

- Specific
  The goal needs to be clearly defined to give you the desired result. If your goals are to diffuse, it is easy to lose your direction and waste resources on unproductive ventures.

- Measurable
  With measurable goals, you can quantify both the progress and the goals themselves, before comparing them to get an indication of your performance and success so far.

- Attainable
  Working on goals that are impossible or too challenging will break your perseverance and determination in the long run. I.e., when defining a goal, be aware of the challenges you will have to overcome to reach that goal. If the challenges turn out to be too big, break the goal into smaller, measurable steps, and work towards it gradually. At the same time, ae aware of setting goals that are to easy to achieve, your goals have to be challenging enough so that you don't slip into the comfort zone and let your progress deteriorate.

- Relevant

  Your goals need to be connected to what you want to achieve. Like unmeasurable goals, irrelevant goals will make you waste time and resources on unproductive tasks.

- Timely

  A deadline is crucial to ensure progress. Without a deadline or a timeframe, you will feel less urgency and motivation to complete the necessary tasks. Your commitment might dwindle and lead to procrastination.

Goal setting not only helps you plan your venture but also makes sure that you are in control of your life as a whole. Smart goal setting ensures that the goals are completed within a timely manner and with the desired outcome.

Why people fail to achieve their goals

- Focusing on long term goals only

  By focusing solely on the end result, it is easy to overlook all the tiny steps necessary to get there. Short term goals are the required stepping stones for realizing the long term goal and will help you focus on building the fundamentals needed for a successful end result.

- Overanalyzing

  Ovaranalyzing generates doubt and can end the goalsetting process in its initial stages. You have to acknowledge that it is not possible to answer all the questions and plan for all contingencies.

- Negative goals

  Goals should be written as something you want to achieve, not something you want to avoid. The way you formulate your goals should serve to inspire you, not instill the fear of failure.

- Unspecific goals

  By creating unspecific goals, it is hard to identify the directions and steps needed to achieve your desired result. This will, in turn, affect both your motivation and perseverance negatively.

- Irrelevant goals

  Spending time and energy on irrelevant goals will severely hurt your overall progress. Identify and work towards the goals that take you where you want to go.

- Unrealistic goals

  If you set goals which you could not realistically achieve within the set timeframe or with your current resources, you will get discouraged and more likely to give up.

  Remember that your short term goals are the stepping stones for your bigger goals and that very few goals are unrealistic if you split them into the necessary short term goals.

- Failing to measure progress

  Measuring your progress is essential to ensure that you're on the right track. Without a way to assess your progress or direction, you can continue in the wrong direction for a long time before realizing you took the wrong turn.

Chapter 3

Your Business Plan

Everybody is motivated by different factors, and you need to develop a plan that is right for you and your business.

Assess your personality, your strengths, and your weaknesses, your overall schedule, and develop a strategy around them.

Be specific about the where, when, and how to execute your plan. Put down points that represent the short term goals and the allotted time.

Be disciplined. If your plan says that you are going to work on a project for two hours every day, work on it for two hours every day.

Make time for reflection every day. Think about what you've done so far, if you need to go over something again and how it has taken you closer to your goal.

Know your market

What does the market need? Who are your main competitors, and which market segments do they serve? What makes your competitors successful? What products or services do they sell, and how can you do it better? If you don't know the answer to these questions, you need to find out. Not knowing the market will stop you before you even begin.

Know your customers

You need to know your customers, what they desire, and how to find them. What are your potential customer's immediate needs? Why do they need the product or service you provide? The type of business you have will determine your target customers, and you need to analyze thoroughly to be sure that you have found your target group.

By targeting the right customers, you will make a better percentage of conversion because your potential buyers already want the unique product or service that you provide.

Know your product

What aspects of your customer's needs do your product or service provider for? Identify your product's key features and how they apply to your customers.

Overcoming obstacles

During every pursuit, you'll face obstacles in one way or another. When working towards a goal, you are not always rewarded with fortune and success. Setbacks can knock people down, but remember that challenges are an integral part of the journey and will make you worthy of eventual triumph.

When meeting an obstacle, you have to deal with it with perseverance and creativity.

- Find out why you are stuck. What prevents you from working through the problem? Break the problem into smaller steps and start thinking outside of the box. Are there other ways to approach the problem? Other people with a different skill set you can lean on? Can you solve parts of the problem yourself and then ask for help? Or, can you reach your goal without dealing with the problem?

- Have you encountered similar problems in the past? How did you solve it then? Can you apply the same or a similar strategy now? Do you know anybody who has solved the same problem in the past?

- Find your strengths. The first steps towards clearing your problem are positive thinking. A positive mindset will make you focus on the end result and force you to find another solution. Which skills do you have to beat the problem? How much effort are you willing to put in? Can you quickly learn a new skill that will assist with solving the problem?

If you can't find a solution at all, put it on hold for a bit and work on other tasks. With time you will get new insight, and new opportunities might present themselves.

Developing a plan

When you have enough knowledge about the market, your product or service, and your potential customers, it is time to create your plan.

Look at your goals (long term and short term) and write a step-by-step plan for achieving your short term goals, and ultimately your primary objectives. Write down how each step will benefit or bring you closer to your desired end result. If you find that the goal is not beneficial, modify or discard it.

Allocate sufficient time and go into details for every step. Identify your resources and try to foresee any potential obstacles and how to overcome them. Are there any areas you'll need to strengthen? Or do you need to hire help?

Identify which areas your talents and abilities are best suited and which you should delegate or outsource.

Potential obstacles you may face:

- Having to little time.

- Not enough money.

- Not having the required knowledge or skills.

- Lack of motivation.

Obstacles don't need to stop you from achieving your goals, but you need to devise a strategy to overcome them.

Make a list of requirements and deadlines for each step and use the short term goals as benchmarks to ensure steady progress towards your longterm goals.

Business Plan Timeline

Create a timeline that brings all your business goals together.

1. Yearly plan:

   Create a general outline for the whole year with your long term plan as your target. Summarize what you will need to do every month to reach your goals and any benchmarks or deadlines you need to complete along the way.

2. Monthly plan:

   Before every month, determine what you need to accomplish that month and write down what you need to do every week to reach your monthly target.

3. Weekly plan:

   Every week, determine and make a list of everything you need to accomplish that week. Break the weekly goals into daily objectives and put them on your daily to-do. Remember to allocate some space on your to-do list in case of delays or other unanticipated problems that need your attention. Use a business appointment planner to quickly get an overview of every day.

4. Daily plan: Use your to-do list as your daily schedule. Prioritize and do the most important tasks first.

43

Designing your business plan

The business plan shall prove that the business is viable for bankers and investors, and are crucial to operating successfully. There are several ways to formulate a business plan. Below I have outlined a basic business plan that you can expand on it as needed. Remember to streamline your writing to get your point across quickly and concisely.

1. Description

    A description of your business, your products and services, and marketing strategy. Try to define what is unique about your business and your products or services. Doing this will help the company stand out and be more appealing to customers.

2. Market analysis

    Describe the marked (size, demographics, potential sales) you are entering and how you will provide your products or services to your customers. Find and analyze your main competitors and how you will promote your business. Describe potential challenges and obstacles and how you plan to overcome them.

3. Organization structure

   Describe how you plan to organize and structure your business. Make a list of all the people involved, their roles, and their qualifications. If you need to acquire additional people or skills, write that as well.

4. Products and services

   Give a description of your products and services. List your suppliers and availability.

5. Marketing

   Describe how you will allow your business to concentrate its resources on the most significant market opportunities.

6. Financial information

   Write down an overview of the economic viability of your business (revenues, expenses, and profits). You don't need to write down your budget in your business plan. Use a Business Budget Planner or a PC app for your main budget.

Fear of Acting

Sometimes the toughest part is acting upon our goals. We don't really know where to start, and it is difficult to see precisely where we will end up. Even with the whole thing planned out, it can be challenging to truly take the leap. There is always one additional thing you could do or something you should have done differently. Very often, the reason is fear. Fear of the unknown and fear of failure.

Fear is understandable. By taking the leap, you are venturing into the unknown. Unfortunately, concerns and uncertainty are part of the process. To achieve great things, you need to challenge your fears. To overcome them, try to write down each fear you have and the possible consequences of failure. By getting your worries down on paper and analyzing them, you will often find that they are exaggerated or unlikely to materialize.

Furthermore, to reduce the chance of your fears to come true, you should make contingency plans you can utilize to prevent or diminish the negative consequences in case your plan goes wrong.

Examples of fears and contingency plans can be:

- Don't quit your day job until your business has turned profitable. By keeping your day job, you know that you can support your financial commitments even if your plan fails.

- Involve your family and loved ones in your project. Explain to them how much it means for you and win their support. Discuss your business thoroughly with your partner and set aside enough money before you start your project.

- Fair of failure. Realize that everybody fails at one point or another. What matters is that you get up again and brush it off. Acknowledge that the possibility of failure is an integral part of being an entrepreneur.

So what is holding you back from achieving success? Failure is not a bad thing. Everybody makes mistakes, and learning from our failures is a fundamental part of being an entrepreneur.

By buying and reading this book, you already have a strong desire to do it, and you should already have defined your goals and created your plan. Your next step is simply to take action!

The First Step

Successful people aren't smarter or more gifted than others, they just to the groundwork and follow through on their plan. They complete all the small steps that eventually make their goal a reality. You simply have to pick a starting point and go from there.

After taking the first step, all subsequent steps will seem easy, and soon you will feel like you're running toward your goal.

Aside from knowing your priorities, it is just as important to use a system to efficiently keep track of your journey. Use your journal to look back on your progress when you feel discouraged, and the endgame seems elusive. When you look back at your progress so far, and the challenges you had to surpass to get to where you are today, you will clearly see that there is a way around every obstacle as long as you dare to face them.

No matter how discouraged you may feel, looking back at prior achievements can help you maintain your perspective and desire to continue.

If you can keep up your motivation, the rest should come with relative ease. Just follow your plan and keep an eye on the goal. Remember to take one thing at the time, from the beginning to the end.

Chapter 4

Time Management

The more you can accomplish, the higher are your chances of success. Time is, therefore, the most valuable resource you have as an entrepreneur.

To be a successful entrepreneur, you need to understand how to manage your time effectively. Proper time management is also beneficial for your mental and physical health and gives you a sense of control and satisfaction. When you are in control of your life, you'll feel more productive and satisfied.

Proper time management requires that you develop a list of tasks, with specific timeframes, that you have to accomplish during your day. Having a proper plan that helps you manage your time will increase your productivity and help you reach your goals in the shortest time possible.

By learning time management skills, you will have a better chance of succeeding, reduce stress, and increase your energy levels. Through proper time management, you can maintain the perfect balance between your work, family, and personal time.

There are several schools of thought when it comes to time management. It is not necessary to know them all or jump into the most advanced ones. You have to find the techniques that fit you and your life best.

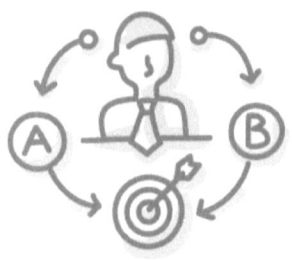

Coordinate your Day

When starting a business, it is easy to be overwhelmed by information, meetings and diversions. It is, therefore, important to not lose sight of the essential details and to stay 100 % focused on the task at hand. Don't check your phone, surf the internet or get lost in irrelevant thoughts.

There is a mountain of things you should or could do every day. Attempting to do them all, you will exhaust yourself and make sure that you do none of them good enough. Instead, focus on a few significant tasks each day (or during a specified timeframe). If you have a lot to do, use your morning to select and order a few tasks by their importance. This makes sure that you do the most critical tasks first and with the maximum energy.

If you over several days or periods find that you have to do more tasks than what you successfully can complete yourself, it is time to look after somebody to assist you grow your business (or outsource some work).

1. Use your journal and to-do list daily.

2. Prioritize your tasks. Determine which tasks are essential and determine a deadline for when they must be completed. Mark all tasks according to importance.

3. Set a timeframe for each task and take regular breaks as you work. Most people can't work efficiently without proper breaks. For maximum productivity, work for 45 minutes before taking a 15-minute break. During your break, you should go to the toilet, eat a meal or do something completely unconnected to your task. This will ensure that you will be able to have full focus during your working phase.

4. Clear your inbox at the end of your day. If someone has taken the time to connect with you, you need to show them that you value their time and effort. It will show your coworkers and partners that you are accessible and ready every day.

5. Put in some available space in your schedule every day. There is always something that comes up that you need to address during the day. If not, take some well deserved time off or work on a recreative activity.

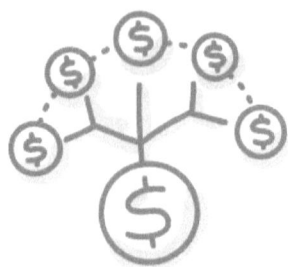

Prioritize and make a To-Do list

A daily to-do list makes it simple to prioritize your tasks and maintain your schedule for the day.

Use the ABCDE-method to prioritize your tasks. Analyze each task for the day and organize them according to importance. Delay or delegate the least important tasks.

> A. Things you need to do.
> B. Things you should do.
> C. Things you could do.
> D. Things you can delegate.
> E. Things you don't need to do.

When scheduling, be sure to also include family time, recreation, enough time for meals and exercise.

When making your to-do list, remember to:

- Keep it simple! There is only so much you can do in one day.

- Start the list with the most critical tasks (i.e., the tasks you must to do) and construct your day around them. Even if the rest of the list stays untouched, the critical stuff will get done.

- Specify your tasks. General terms such as "work" is too vague, instead, break the work into smaller and more specific steps with as much information as possible.

- Time your list. When your list is done, go back and put a time estimate next to every task or step. For more efficient list writing, you could use a business appointment planner.

- Be flexible with your planning. In case something unforeseen occurs or you need some time off work, leave 10-15 minutes of open space between the tasks so you won't break your schedule.

At the end of each day, stop and think:

- What did I achieve today? How did it take me closer to my goal?

- Do I need to do something different tomorrow?

Know when to Delegate

At some point, you will realize that you are not able to do everything yourself. You might not have enough time to do specific tasks, or you will encounter barriers that need qualifications you don't have. You only have a selected number of hours each day, so don't use them on tasks that don't need your specific attention or you don't have the qualifications to do correctly.

Start by analyzing and deciding which tasks should be delegated or outsourced and how you want them completed. Be clear about how it needs to be done, when it must be completed, and the required result.

Before delegating or outsourcing a job, ask yourself the following questions:

- Which tasks can be delegated?

- Which steps are needed to complete the task?

- What is the desired result and timeframe?

- Who is the most competent person to complete the task?

If you need to outsource, there are a few freelance websites where you can find the talent you need:

- Fiverr
  On Fiverr, you can buy services know as "Gigs." Fiverr is one of the world's largest digital marketplaces, and prices start at a very reasonable rate of $5. You can buy more expensive gigs according to your needs.

- Upwork
  Upwork specializes in connecting clients with freelancers. The freelancers can be bought for entire projects or on an hourly basis. Upwork makes it easy to track your freelancer's progress, and you can pay after the project is done.

Take Frequent Breaks

Working too much leads to unhappiness and burnouts. Stress can add up faster than you think, and neglecting to take regular breaks is one of the greatest mistakes you can make as a new entrepreneur. Every now and then, you need to take a break and recharge your body and mind. Just a few moments on the couch or outside to clear your mind will do wonders for your health.

When at home, relax and spend some quality time with your family and friends. Eat an overall healthy diet to restore your energy levels and exercise regularly. Pursue a hobby or recreational activity that allows you to take your mind off work.

The same goes for vacations and weekends off. You don't need to put off work completely every weekend or for weeks at a time, but every now and then, your family, friends, or a recreational activity should be your primary focus.

Chapter 5

Productivity

Effectiveness is about the big picture and doing the right things. It is when your actions are in line with your main goal. By being effective, you are productive and work on ways to improve your outcomes, and not waste time on irrelevant tasks that do not serve your goals.

To be more effective, focus on the goals you want to achieve and find the critical strategies needed for success.

Efficiency is more about doing things right. It is doing something as perfect as possible in the least amount of time possible while at the same time being cost-efficient. You can be effective without being efficient and vice versa, and it is not possible to reach peak productivity if you lack in either of them.

Once you have laid out the basics, you can then look at how you can improve the way you do things. The key is to make sure you are efficient at the tasks that are most important in supporting your goals.

Avoid Procrastination

Procrastination is a time thief that should be avoided at all costs. To help you avoid procrastination, you can try some of the following tips.

1. Adhere to your to-do list deadlines and schedule.

2. Keep your work desk clean and your room without distractions.

3. Identify time thieves (social networks, apps, games, etc.) and remove them.

Self-discipline

One trait shared by many successful entrepreneurs are that they have immense self-discipline. It takes a high level of self-discipline to maintain your motivation when meeting difficulty after difficulty. When things get tough, self-discipline will be the characteristic that carries you through to victory.

Self-discipline is the ability to keep focus on what needs to be done (instead of what you want to do). To not let your impulses or feelings influence your choices.

Your level of self-discipline is a result of the life you have lived so far and you can improve your self-discipline throughout your life. To become more self-disciplined, try to identify your weaknesses and shortcomings and take the necessary steps to improve.

Improving yourself in any area will not only make you better or teach you new skills, it will also naturally develop your self-discipline.

Focus

In a fast-paced world surrounded by technology, we are constantly multitasking. You might be able to do several tasks at once, but it makes it impossible to concentrate fully on all of them. By cutting or delegating the less important tasks, you can give your full attention to the ones that matter the most.

In addition to a healthy lifestyle, there are two rules you should follow:

1. Don't multitask: Doing more does not translate to better results. Delegate as needed and focus on the essential tasks only you can do.

2. Stick to your schedule: Work for 50 minutes and then take a 10-minute break. Avoid procrastination at all costs. If you get overwhelmed by work, scale back to ensure that the work you do is of high quality.

Tools and apps to help you increase your Productivity

There are thousands of productivity and time management tools and apps that you can use to help you manage your time and be more efficient.

The following apps are well tested and will help you significantly improve your productivity.

Google Calendar

Google Calendar (https://calendar.google.com) is a great way to maintain your schedule. Google Calendar is free and can be used from anywhere. If you work with a team, it is easy to share plans between all team members.

RescueTime

RescueTime (https://www.rescuetime.com) will help you understand your daily habits so that you can focus on the essential ones. RescueTime runs as a background app on your PC or mobile devices and tracks how much time you spend on different applications and websites. With RescueTime, you can block distracting websites and see how much time you've spent reading and responding to emails.

Focus Booster

Focus Booster (http://www.focusboosterapp.com) can help you understand how you spend your time by visualizing your progress. The app can also generate invoices and reports you can share with your clients.

Toggl

Toggl (https://www.toggl.com) is a time tracking app that helps you see how much time you spend on different projects. This will show you what tasks are making you money and which ones are holding you back.

Evernote

Evernote (https://www.evernote.com) is a complete productivity tool where you can record meetings, notes, interviews, and ideas. Evernote is cloud-based and lets you share all your files with the rest of the team.

Mindmeister

Mindmeister (https://www.mindmeister.com) is an online mind mapping tool that can help you organize your thoughts and ideas.

MyLifeOrganized

MyLifeOrganized (https://www.mylifeorganized.com) is a task management tool that will help you target what you should be focusing on to reach your daily objectives.

If you prefer to do your planning and journaling by paperback, Ibenholt Books have a series of Business Planner books. All books are made for starting entrepreneurs and small businesses.

I especially recommend the Business Appointment Planner, which is perfect for easy and efficient to-do lists and daily scheduling.

Business Planner (viewbook.at/businessplanner)
A professional Business Planner can help you manage your business with yearly, monthly, and weekly spreads, inventory lists, marketing notes, and much more.

Business Sales Organizer (viewbook.at/salesorganizer)
A sales organizer is a great way to organize all your sales by order date, number, and profit.

Business Inventory Logbook (viewbook.at/inventorylogbook)
A logbook that will help you keep track of your inventory. Contain date, product and product quantity, cost, and more.

Business Appointment Planner (viewbook.at/appointmentplanner)
The appointment planner will help you organize and keep track of all your appointments. The appointment book is also an excellent tool for to-do lists.

Business Contacts Book (viewbook.at/businesscontacts)

Great help if you have a lot of business contacts, suppliers, etc. This book also lets you write extended notes on each contact.

Notes

Notes

Notes

Notes

Notes

Notes

Notes

Notes

Notes

Notes

Notes

Notes

Notes

Notes

Notes

Notes

Notes

Notes

Notes

Notes

Notes

Notes

Notes

Notes

Notes

Notes

Notes

Notes

Notes

Notes

Notes

Notes

Notes

Notes

Notes

Notes

Notes

Notes

Notes

www.ingramcontent.com/pod-product-compliance
Lightning Source LLC
Chambersburg PA
CBHW030722220526
45463CB00005B/2137